PLASTIC

• KNOW YOUR FACTS • TAKE ACTION • SAVE THE OCEANS

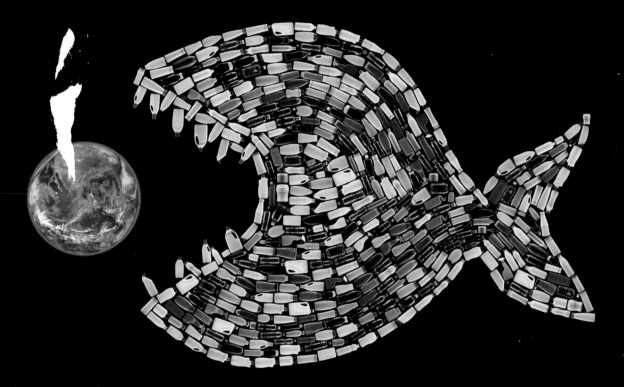

by Ruth Owen

With thanks to

Dr. Sue Kinsey

Senior Pollution Policy Officer

Marine Conservation Society

RUBY TUESDAY BOOKS

Published in 2019 by Ruby Tuesday Books Ltd.

Editor: Mark J. Sachner
Designer: Emma Randall
Production: John Lingham

Photo credits:
Alamy: Cover, 6 (right), 7 (bottom right), 9 (bottom), 21 (top left); Evoware: 25 (top); FLPA: 6 (left), 8, 9 (centre), 20 (top), 21 (centre); Hubbub.org.uk: 22 (top); Istock Photo: 13 (bottom); NASA: 4—5, 17 (bottom) Goddard Space Flight Center Scientific Visualization Studio; Nature Picture Library: 4 (top), 5 (centre), 28 (centre left); The Ocean Cleanup: 23; Public Domain: 5 (bottom); Ruby Tuesday Books: 12 (bottom), 13 (top right), 16 (bottom), 17 (top); Shutterstock: Cover, 1, 4 (bottom), 5 (top), 7 (top), 7 (bottom left), 9 (top), 10—11, 12 (top), 13 (centre), 14—15, 16 (top), 17 (centre), 18—19, 20 (bottom), 21 (top right), 21 (bottom), 22 (bottom), 24, 26—27, 28 (top), 28 (centre right), 28 (bottom), 29, 30 (top), 30 (centre), 31; Skipping Rocks Lab: 25 (bottom); Washedashore.org: 30 (bottom).
Alamy: Cover, 6 (right), 7 (bottom right), 9 (bottom), 21 (top left); Evoware: 25 (top); FLPA: 6 (left), 8, 9 (centre), 20 (top), 21 (centre); Hubbub.org.uk: 22 (top); Istock Photo: 13 (bottom); NASA: 4—5, 17 (bottom) Goddard Space Flight Center Scientific Visualization Studio; Nature Picture Library: 4 (top), 5 (centre), 28 (centre left); The Ocean Cleanup: 23; Public Domain: 5 (bottom); Ruby Tuesday Books: 12 (bottom), 13 (top right), 16 (bottom), 17 (top); Shutterstock: Cover, 1, 4 (bottom), 5 (top), 7 (top), 7 (bottom left), 9 (top), 10—11, 12 (top), 13 (centre), 14—15, 16 (top), 17 (centre), 18—19, 20 (bottom), 21 (top right), 21 (bottom), 22 (bottom), 24, 26—27, 28 (top), 28 (centre right), 28 (bottom), 29, 30 (top), 30 (centre), 31; Skipping Rocks Lab: 25 (bottom); Washedashore.org: 30 (bottom).

ISBN 978-1-78856-078-8

Printed in Poland by L&C Printing Group

www.rubytuesdaybooks.com

Contents

Our Blue Planet

A tiny blue dot. A blue marble. The blue planet. All these phrases perfectly describe the place that we call home. From space, our Earth looks blue because 71 percent of its surface is covered with oceans.

A sealion plays with her pup in a forest of kelp.

A titan triggerfish feeds on coral.

Just **1 litre** of seawater contains **38,000** different species of **microbes**.

A turtle hatchling climbs from an underground nest on a sandy beach. Instinct tells her to run to the sea. If she stays healthy and safe, the turtle may live for up to 80 years.

The Longest Swim

Every year, gray whales make a 16,000-kilometre migration. They swim south from their feeding grounds in the cold Arctic seas to warm Pacific waters off the coast of California and Mexico. The whales meet up to mate and females that are already pregnant give birth. Then the giant animals make the long swim back to the icy north.

The Air We Breathe

Just like plants on land, microscopic, plant-like phytoplankton produce oxygen. Scientists estimate that phytoplankton in Earth's oceans produce about half of the oxygen in our atmosphere.

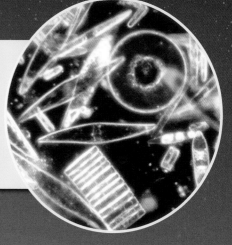

No one knows how many different species of living things are in the ocean. Scientists have identified and named more than 240,000. However, there are likely to be millions more.

Every single one, no matter how big or small, depends on Earth's oceans for survival. But the oceans are in trouble.

Big trouble. . . .

Our Plastic Planet

Every year up to **13 million tonnes** of plastic enters the world's oceans.

It's such an enormous number, it's impossible to imagine it. But break it down, and it looks like 60 trucks piled high with plastic bags, water bottles and other rubbish emptying their cargo into the sea . . .

. . . EVERY hour . . .

. . . day and night . . .

. . . 365 days of the year.

A sealion tangled in a plastic fishing net spends her days in terrible agony.

A titan triggerfish swims on a coral reef feeding on plastic that it thinks is food.

A turtle swallows a plastic bag, thinking it's a jellyfish.

Not Just One Life

A turtle's stomach can become clogged with plastic bags. Then, unable to eat real food, it starves to death. Once the turtle's body rots, the plastic bags are released back into the ocean to kill again. When a female turtle dies, it's not just one life lost to the ocean. All the hundreds of babies she would have produced during her long life are lost, too.

This gray whale calf has become entangled in plastic fishing lines.

A single plastic bottle breaks up into thousands of tiny pieces. That's enough to put a piece on every kilometre of beach in the world!

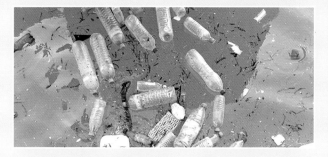

The Mariana Trench in the Pacific is the deepest part of the world's oceans. Even here there is plastic – 11 kilometres down!

If a whale can't swim to the surface to breathe, it will drown.

It's easy to see some of the terrible harm that ocean plastic causes. But most is hidden from view. And the level of pollution is escalating so fast, there may be problems ahead that we've not yet imagined. . . .

A Story of Plastic

An albatross dances with her mate. Moving gracefully, they copy each other in a dance they have performed together for more than 30 years.

Many albatrosses will mate for life. They may live for more than 60 years.

The albatrosses spend most of their lives out at sea. But each year they return to Midway Island in the Pacific Ocean to mate and raise a chick.

The mother albatross lays her single egg in a sandy nest. Then the parents take it in turns to incubate the egg for around 65 days.

It can take up to two days for an albatross chick to hatch. As it struggles to break from its shell, the parents softly sing to it.

Once their chick hatches, the parents must bring it food.

The mother albatross flies out to sea. She scoops up fish eggs, squid and other food from the surface of the water.

tiny pieces of jagged, broken plastic

bottle tops

plastic toys

toothbrushes

A parent albatross may be out at sea catching food for up to a week. During this time, it flies around 16,000 kilometres.

When she returns, the mother bird regurgitates an oily, fishy mixture into her hungry chick's beak. But she doesn't realise that some of the colourful mixture she has brought back is plastic and will be deadly to her chick.

Day after day, the albatrosses work hard to care for their baby. But each meal they bring is slowly killing the little chick.

Plastic objects can block a chick's intestines. Sharp pieces of plastic may pierce or tear its insides. Eventually, a chick's stomach becomes so full of plastic there's no room for real food and it starves to death.

This dead chick's stomach is filled with plastic.

Every year, **thousands** of **albatross chicks** are **killed** by **plastic**.

Problem Plastics

Plastic was a truly incredible invention. From crash helmets to seatbelts, computers to footballs, it has been used in thousands of ways that make our lives safer and more enjoyable.

However, not all plastic objects are made to be used again and again.

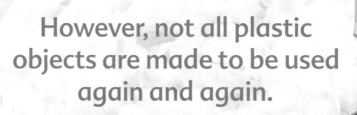

Today, our world is filled with **single-use plastics**. These plastic objects are designed to be used **only once**.

A plastic bottle is forever, not just for Christmas!

Almost a quarter of the plastic that washes up on beaches in many parts of the world is ON THE GO LITTER such as plastic cutlery, cups and bottles. We use these things to make eating and drinking more convenient for us, but they become deadly hazards for ocean animals that think they are food.

Would you want to eat someone else's rubbish?

Does it make sense to wrap foods that have tough, protective skins in plastic?

Every country has its own mind-boggling statistics for single-use plastics. In the UK, 36 million single-use plastic bottles are used each day. About 14.5 million of these are littered, go into landfill or are incinerated (burned) to make electricity.

Isn't it just a little crazy to use a material that may last forever to make something that will be used for just a few minutes?

No Such Thing as AWAY

Most of the plastic that's ever been produced is still out there somewhere in our world. When we throw plastic away, there's no such thing as AWAY!

Together Forever?

If you bury an apple core in the ground it breaks down, becoming water, natural gases and minerals. Nothing harmful is left behind. If you bury a plastic bottle, it breaks up. Over many, many years it cracks and crumbles into smaller and smaller pieces. However, the plastic is still there in the ground – even if the powder-like pieces are too small to see.

When plastic is thrown away, it can end up buried in landfill. It may be out of sight, but it will never be gone!

Layers of soil

Plastic sheets

- Plastics and other rubbish in landfill release chemicals that mix with rainwater.
- Thick plastic sheets stop this toxic mixture polluting the surrounding soil.
- If the plastic sheets split, polluting liquids can escape. Then they may trickle under the ground and eventually flow into streams, rivers and the ocean.

Is Recycling the Answer?

Recycling helps. But today we use so much plastic, recycling simply can't keep up!

REJECTED!

Many plastics are too difficult or expensive to recycle. These items get put in the dustbin and can't be sent for recycling.

Clingfilm

Black plastic trays

Plastic contaminated with food

Styrofoam takeaway boxes

Plastic sleeves and wraps

HEINZ BEANZ

LIQUID SOAP
Dispenser Pump Bottle
COSMETIC

Plastic that's combined with another material, such as bottle pumps that contain metal

Plastic from a recycled bottle doesn't usually become a new bottle. That's because the plastic loses its quality once it's recycled. The new, low-quality plastic is used to make carpets or stuffing for sofas. When these items are no longer wanted, they will end up in landfill.

Someone Else's Problem?

Countries such as the UK and USA can no longer process all the plastic that's collected for recycling. Therefore, recycling companies export the material to Asia and other parts of the world. Often, the plastic waste is not suitable for recycling or there's simply too much. Overwhelmed by tonnes of someone else's waste, recycling companies have no choice but to bury, burn or even dump the plastic. This means our rubbish is polluting another person's country – thousands of kilometres away. It may even end up in the ocean!

A Journey to the Ocean

Billions of plastic objects are polluting the world's oceans. But how did they get there?

1 A person litters by throwing away a plastic bag in the street.

2 The plastic bag gets blown here and there by the wind.

3 In time, the bag is blown into a river.

4 The river flows into the sea, and the bag goes, too.

97% of **Earth's water** is in the oceans.

Plastic rubbish that's dropped in the street may get washed down a drain with rainwater. The drain leads to a river that will eventually flow into the ocean.

All **rivers** eventually lead to the **sea.**

Plastic from landfills may be blown long distances into a river or to the sea.

Litter on beaches gets blown or washed into the ocean. Bottles, straws and other plastics are dropped into the sea by people on cruise ships, fishing and tourist boats and oil rigs.

Plastic fishing lines and nets are lost or thrown away by people on fishing boats.

The Facts on Flushing

Wet wipes, sanitary towels, tampons, cotton buds and nappies should NEVER be flushed down the toilet. These items can block sewers and many contain plastic that will end up in the sea.

When you flush the toilet, the waste (water, pee, poo, toilet paper and other materials) flows from your home into a network of underground sewer pipes.

The sewers carry the waste to a treatment plant. Here, the waste flows through sieve-like grids to filter out items such as nappies and tampons.

The poo is removed and then the remaining liquid is treated to make it clean and germ free.

Finally, clean water is released from the treatment plant into a river or the sea.

Sometimes, however, small items such as cotton buds and wet wipes get through the filters and escape into the sea.

If there's a blockage in the sewers, waste is released directly into a river or the sea without being filtered or cleaned.

15

Rubbish on the Move

A piece of plastic in the ocean may be carried for thousands of kilometres by ocean currents.

Plastic washes up on beaches in remote places far from where there are people. In Antarctica and the Arctic plastic floats in the icy seas, and has been found frozen into the sea ice.

Not Many People, Lots of Plastic

The Cocos Keeling Islands are a group of 27 small islands in the Indian Ocean. Only two of the islands are inhabited with just 600 people. However, the beaches on all the islands are polluted by plastic. That's because ocean currents carry millions of pieces of plastic from nearby Indonesia and other countries in Asia, such as China and Thailand.

This map shows how ocean currents (in red) flow towards the Cocos Keeling Islands.

Ocean Garbage Patches

Vast areas of circling water, called gyres, form in the Earth's oceans.

North
America

Europe

Asia

Atlantic
Ocean

Africa

Pacific
Ocean

Pacific
Ocean

South
America

Indian
Ocean

Australia

Earth's five major gyres are in the Atlantic, Pacific and Indian oceans.

As ocean currents flow into a gyre, the plastic goes, too. Then it becomes trapped, forming a giant floating rubbish, or garbage, patch.

The water in a garbage patch may contain large objects, such as plastic oil drums and bottles. But most of the plastic is tiny. Trillions of tiny bits of plastic form a disgusting, poisonous plastic soup.

The Great Pacific Garbage Patch in the North Pacific is the largest. It covers an area three times the size of France. Scientists estimate that it contains 1.8 trillion pieces of plastic that weigh the same as 500 jumbo jets.

White lines show the flow of ocean currents in the Atlantic Ocean.

Microplastics

The tiny, often microscopic, pieces of plastic in the ocean are known as microplastics.

Once a bottle, or other plastic object, is in the sea, a combination of sunlight and seawater makes the plastic brittle.

The bottle starts to degrade.

It breaks up into pieces that become smaller . . .

. . . and smaller . . .

. . . and smaller.

Microplastic is any piece of plastic smaller than 5 mm.

It may take up to 450 years for a bottle to become microplastics.

Seabirds, crabs, squid, fish and other animals think microplastics are food and eat them. Pieces of plastic can fill an animal's stomach, making it feel full. Then the animal stops eating and starves to death. Scientists estimate that 9 out of 10 seabirds have plastic in their stomachs.

Plastic may contain toxic chemicals such as dyes. As an object degrades, these pollutants are released into the water. Scientists have also discovered that microplastics soak up chemicals that are already in the sea. When an animal eats microplastics, all these poisons may go into its body.

How Long Is Long?

How long will it take a plastic object to break up into microplastics out at sea? No one can say for sure, but scientists have tried to estimate the length of time for some common items of plastic rubbish.

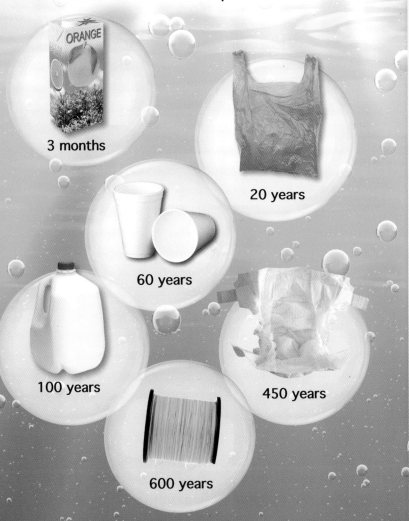

3 months

20 years

60 years

100 years

450 years

600 years

Nurdles are tiny plastic pellets that are melted to make plastic items. Trillions of nurdles get washed down drains at factories. They also spill from trains, trucks and ships during transportation and end up in the sea.

A Plastic Ocean Food Chain

When we eat fish and other seafood, are WE eating microplastics and toxins? The answer is YES! Samples of mussels sold in supermarkets have been found to contain microplastics. And if we eat fish contaminated by toxins from plastic, these chemicals will enter our bodies.

Cod and chips

A big fish, such as a cod, eats the small fish.

Small fish eat microplastics.

Human consumption of plastic is a hot topic and lots more scientific research is needed. Scientists want to understand how much plastic could be in our food and how dangerous it will be.

One Small Action

A problem like plastic pollution can seem overwhelming. It's easy to feel that one person's actions can't possibly make a difference — but they do.

If you're reading this book you're probably not someone who drops litter. But others do.

So take action!

SMALL ACTION:

Pick up someone else's abandoned plastic bottle and recycle it.

BIG RESULTS:

That bottle won't now become thousands of pieces of microplastic floating in the ocean – forever!

Many miles from where you live, an albatross won't feed the bottle's cap to her precious chick.

SMALL ACTION:

See some string or fishing line on a beach, pick it up and throw it away responsibly.

BIG RESULTS:

An animal won't become entangled in the string and die.

Recycle or throw it away.
Wash your hands.
Know you've helped!

SMALL ACTION:

Never flush a cotton bud down the loo.

BIG RESULTS:

Your cotton bud won't head out to sea through the sewers and become a poisonous meal for an animal.

Buy cotton buds with card or bamboo sticks that will rot away in landfill.

SMALL ACTION:

See a plastic bag tangled in a bush. Take it home and put it in the dustbin.

BIG RESULTS:

You've just stopped it blowing out to sea and suffocating a turtle.

✓ Go to a beach
✓ Take 5 minutes
✓ Pick up plastic
✓ Recycle or bin it

 Go with a friend and double your impact!

Every Piece Counts

Around the world thousands of people are taking action by removing plastic from rivers, beaches and the ocean.

Fishing For Plastic

On the River Thames in London the Hubbub charity organises fishing trips with a difference. Clean-up teams take to the water to fish for plastic! The rubbish that's collected is recycled and turned into a material named Plaswood. The Plaswood is made into small boats that are used for trips to collect more plastic from the river.

MADE FROM RECYCLED PLASTIC

Every Piece Counts

Worldwide, people of all ages take part in beach clean-ups. Every piece of plastic that's picked up is one less piece that will be washed back out to sea. Often, the plastic that's collected can be recycled.

Scientists and environmentalists who join beach clean-ups examine the rubbish and analyse where it has come from. If they discover that a company is dumping plastic in the sea, the polluters can be made to stop. Scientists may discover that lots of rubbish is coming from a particular seaside town or beachside resort. Then local conservation groups can start an anti-littering campaign and ask the local council to provide more litter bins.

An Inventor's Story

Boyan Slat is a young inventor who is developing a way to trap plastic in the world's ocean garbage patches.

The Ocean Cleanup system is a U-shaped, floating trap that is carried through the water by ocean currents, waves and the wind.

As the trap moves, plastic on the water's surface and just below is trapped in the system.

Every few months a boat will collect the plastic and take it back to land.

Boyan Slat began work on his idea as a school science project when he was just 16.

In the future, Boyan and his team hope to use Ocean Cleanup systems to remove plastic from the world's gyres.

Wind, waves and current propel the system.

The Ocean Cleanup is 600 metres long.

Plastic gets trapped here.

Useful plastic could be sold for recycling, while low-quality plastic would be burned to make electricity.

Plastic-Free Food & Drink

A banana or an orange is ready-packaged in its own tough skin. We eat the fruit, and then the skin can be composted. What does composting mean?

1
If you bury a banana skin in the ground, nature will take care of it. Insects, fungi and microbes in the soil break it down leaving nothing but nutrients that will feed more plants.

2
Wouldn't it be great if instead of plastic, our food was packaged in materials that could be composted?

3
Scientists and designers are developing packaging materials made from wood, grass, seaweed and mushrooms.

4
Instead of going to landfill, our food packaging would be sent to composting centres. Here, the waste packaging could become compost for feeding crops on farms.

The tomatoes are harvested.

The tomato plant's dead leaves and stalks are mixed with recycled cardboard to make a carton.

A No-Waste Packaging Life Cycle

The compost is used to feed new tomato plants.

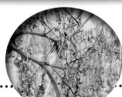

Once the carton is used, it can be composted.

Eat the Packaging

In Indonesia, a company called Evoware are developing packaging made from seaweed. Their packaging dissolves in warm water so it's perfect for single servings of coffee, tea or soup. The seaweed packaging can be used to wrap products such as soap, sweets or burgers. It's even edible, so you can eat the wrapping with your burger!

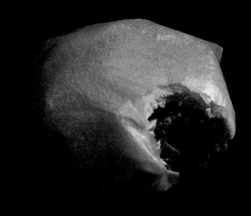

A seaweed-wrapped burger

Sweets in seaweed bags

Evoware's Ello Jello seaweed cup leaves no waste behind. You simply drink your drink and then eat the cup.

The cups can be produced with flavours such as orange or peppermint.

Making Plastic Disappear

In London the Ooho Water team have created a plastic-like membrane (or skin) that holds water. The bite-sized bubbles of water are perfect for people when they are out and about. They can also be used at sporting events, such as marathons, where athletes need a quick drink on the go. Ooho is 100% natural because it's made from seaweed. And there's no waste because it can be swallowed with the water!

If an item needs packaging, the materials must help nature, not harm it. Designers must design with the end in mind!

Going Plastic-Free

We can clean up, invent new kinds of packaging and recycle. But none of this will be enough unless we all start using less plastic. On the next few pages you will find lots of ideas for going plastic-free.

Choose products that are made to last and can be reused again and again. When you need something new, ask yourself:

Can I buy this secondhand?

Feeling thirsty?

Fill a glass with water from a tap or use a drinking fountain. When you're out and about, carry a reusable water bottle.

Use a bar of soap instead of soap in plastic bottles.

Use a flannel instead of wet wipes or plastic sponges.

Cut the clingfilm! Ask everyone in your family to put leftovers into reusable containers.

Gift a Small Change

When it's time to give someone a gift, buy them a reusable water bottle, coffee cup or shopping bag.

When shopping, make plastic-free choices. Glass containers are better than plastic because glass can be recycled again and again without ever losing its quality.

Don't wash glitter down the drain. It will end up in the ocean as microplastic.

When your family is shopping for food, choose loose fruit and vegetables. Avoid putting them into individual small plastic bags. Just carefully pack them into reusable bags that you've brought from home.

Say Bye-Bye to Balloons

NEVER release balloons into the sky. They are made from plastic or latex. Balloons can blow for thousands of miles and end up in the ocean. Once they burst or deflate, animals may eat them thinking they are food. The plastic strings and ribbons on balloons can entangle and kill animals.

Around the world, plastic straws and cutlery are being banned. Start your own ban NOW, and when you're offered these items, just say NO!

A turtle or whale may think a burst balloon is a tasty squid.

ON THE GO Litter

Make your own food and carry it in a reusable box. Avoid buying sandwiches and other foods packed in single-use plastic.

More Plastic-Free Ideas

You probably already recycle as much as possible. But how about recycling less?

Take the Recycling Challenge

Once you try to cut single-use plastic from your life, you'll have less to recycle.

Take a look at how much plastic goes into your family's recycling bin or box each week. Set your family a challenge. By buying and using less single-use plastic, can you reduce the amount you need to recycle by half in three months?

Spring the Trap!

If you can't recycle plastic can holders cut them up before putting them in the dustbin. This will stop animals getting trapped in them.

REMEMBER! Only flush the 3 Ps

The only things that should be flushed down the toilet are Pee, Poo and Paper. Unlike wet wipes, cotton buds and other non-flushables, toilet paper is designed to break up into tiny pieces so it doesn't cause blockages in sewers. Also, toilet paper is made from wood, so it's natural and breaks down once it's in water.

Brush With Bamboo

Plastic toothbrushes regularly end up in the ocean and can be deadly to animals that think they're food. Dentists recommend that we change our toothbrushes every 12 weeks. That means we may each be throwing away four brushes a year. Buy a toothbrush with a bamboo handle. Then, once your old brush goes to landfill, the bamboo will eventually rot away just like any other natural plant matter.

Ask Questions Be Informed

While recycling isn't the perfect solution to the problem of plastic, it's still worth doing all we can. Find out as much information as possible from your local council about what can and can't be recycled in your area.

Ask For Change

Don't be afraid to challenge the companies whose brands you buy. If you're unhappy about the amount of plastic packaging they use, contact them by email or social media and tell them! Ask them WHEN they are going to make changes.

Grow Your Own

Herbs make food taste great. But when we buy them from supermarkets, they're often wrapped in plastic. Buy some seeds, follow the instructions on the packet and grow your own herbs in recycled containers made from yogurt pots, plastic bottles and even egg boxes.

Plastic Microfibres

Some fabrics, such as polyester, are made from plastics. When an item of clothing made from this kind of fabric is washed, up to 2000 tiny fibres can be released. The fibres travel from the washing machine, into the sewers and out to sea. Then they become part of the microplastics problem.

Whenever possible, choose clothes made from natural fabrics such as cotton or wool. Tiny fibres from these clothes will break down and rot away in water.

29

Everything You Do Counts

Become a Revolting Shopper!

If you don't want the plastic that's wrapped around your food in a supermarket, revolt! Remove the plastic and take it to the Customer Services Desk. Politely explain that you're not happy about the amount of plastic waste and you'd like the shop to dispose of it for you. Ask if your feedback can also be passed on to the store's Head Office.

Your Name Has Power

You may not be old enough to vote – yet – but by signing online petitions, making pledges and joining campaigns on social media, your name will count. Petitions can be presented to large companies, such as fast food chains, to show them that their customers are unhappy about the amount of throwaway plastic they produce.

If you don't live near the sea, you can still pick up litter from the street, a park or by a river. Litter in these places can be blown long distances and end up in the ocean.

Make Art!

In Oregon, USA, the helpers and artists of the Washed Ashore project clean up beaches and use the plastic waste to create giant animal sculptures. The sculptures are used to educate and inspire people to make changes and reduce their plastic use. Try turning your family or school's plastic waste into a piece of art instead of throwing it away.

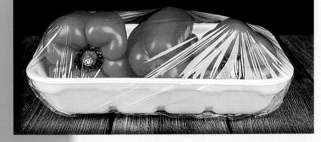

Passing It On

Before you buy something plastic, such as a toy, gadget or piece of jewellery, think about the end of its life. Will you be able to pass it on to a friend or give it to a charity shop when you're tired of it?

Spread the Word

Tell everyone about plastic pollution. The facts are upsetting and hard to forget. Your family and friends may not change what they do overnight, but each time they go to buy something plastic, your voice will be niggling in the back of their mind. And if they feel guilty about their purchase and make a different choice, you've just helped to save the oceans!

Consumer Power

As a consumer (the person who buys or uses something) you have power. When you stop buying a plastic product, the shop and manufacturer loses a sale. If large numbers of customers do this, these companies will see their sales drop. You will reduce the spread of plastic and send a powerful message to big businesses.

A Message to You

Right now, you're probably feeling as if a lot of older people out there have made a huge mess of the world. And you're right – we have!

However, large numbers of us really do care. We love nature, animals and our wonderful planet and like you, we want to do all we can to put things right. Everyone can do something, and lots of small actions can have big results.

The fight back is underway . . .

Ruby Tuesday Books

31

Glossary

compostable
Able to be broken down by nature into water, gases and minerals, while leaving nothing harmful behind.

current
A movement of water in a stream, river, lake or ocean.

degrade
To break down or reduce in quality.

landfill
A place where a large quantity of rubbish is buried in the ground to get rid of it.

microbes
Living things that are too tiny to see without a microscope. Some microbes are helpful, while others, such as germs, can be harmful.

microplastics
Tiny pieces of plastic that are less than 5 mm long.

pollution
Rubbish, liquids, gases or other substances and materials that are harmful to living things and to the land, water and air.

sewers
Large pipes that carry waste from homes and other buildings to treatment plants where the waste is made safe.

single-use plastics
Plastic objects that are made to be used just once.

Index